GW00420418

VICTORIAN NEEDLEPOINT DESIGNS

from Godey's Lady's Book
and Peterson's Magazine

Edited by Rita Weiss

Dover Publications, Inc., New York

Copyright © 1975 by Dover Publications, Inc.
All rights reserved under Pan American and International Copyright Conventions.

Published in Canada by General Publishing Company,
Ltd., 30 Lesmill Road, Don Mills, Toronto, Ontario.
Published in the United Kingdom by Constable and
Company, Ltd., 10 Orange Street, London WC 2.

This Dover edition, first published in 1975, is a new collection of designs for needlepoint selected from "Godey's Lady's Book" and "Peterson's Magazine", 1852-1880.

International Standard Book Number: 0-486-23163-1
Library of Congress Catalog Card Number: 74-24489

Manufactured in the United States of America
Dover Publications, Inc.
180 Varick Street
New York, N.Y. 10014

Introduction

The needleworker who has tired of working designs from mass-produced needlepoint and embroidery kits will find in this book a wealth of new ideas for creative projects. Originally printed in the late nineteenth century in the two most important women's magazines of that era, *Godey's Lady's Book* and *Peterson's Magazine,* the designs are all readily adaptable to today's needlework.

Many of the patterns were originally intended for "Berlin work," a term which was applied to all types of needlework on canvas during the Victorian era. The name is derived from the fact that the original charted patterns and brightly colored wools used for this work came from Berlin. Often the patterns were handpainted to match the subtle shadings of the wools, and the color plates were individually tipped into the magazines. Birds, floral designs and deer were extremely popular subjects, and in executing them the needleworker often employed several different stitches on the dark background that was used for almost all needlepoint in the nineteenth century. The design on page 36 is an example of a Berlin pattern, and the inside and back covers show Berlin patterns in color.

Berlin work continued to be the most popular needlework fashion from the mid-1850's until the end of the century. Not only did the typical Victorian parlor contain chair seats, pillows and stools covered with Berlin work, it was also filled with Berlin work pictures, screens, banners and lamp mats. As traveling became more and more popular, all kinds of Berlin work traveling accessories began to be made. Victorian ladies always carried their "railway bags," needlepointed from Berlin patterns. The design on the back cover of this book was intended to be made up into a Berlin work "railway bag." Even wearing apparel—from men's suspenders to dainty slippers—was decorated with Berlin work. The designs on pages 22–25 were, in fact, originally intended to be used on needlepoint slippers. They have been enlarged here to make them more legible.

Other designs in this book were originally intended to be executed in "Java canvas work." This involved an embroidery technique similar to counted-thread embroidery; patterns being worked from charts in large open stitches over "Java canvas," a loosely woven, even-meshed linen or cotton cloth that also served as background. Java canvas designs were fairly bold, and did not feature the subtle shadings often found in Berlin work. The finished embroidery was generally made up into a "tidy," a piece of fancy work to protect the back or arms of upholstery. The needle-point pillow on the cover, made from the Java canvas design that appears on page 4, is an example of how well these patterns work up in needlepoint.

A few of the designs included in this collection were patterns for "darning on square netting." In this technique the needleworker used a very intricate process for making square netting and then, working from a chart, orna-mented the netting with a pattern in darning. As the resulting handiwork was a rather flimsy piece of embroidery, these designs were intended primarily for curtains or tidies. The hanging basket on page 18 is a design for darning on square netting.

Since all of the patterns are marked on a grid, each square in the grid representing a stitch to be taken, the designs may be worked directly onto needlepoint canvas by counting off on it the same number of warp and woof squares shown in the diagram. To determine how large the finished piece will be, measure the number of squares in the design If you are using a #12 canvas, and the chart shows twelve squares for each inch, your twelve stitches will measure one inch. If you are using a #5 or a #10 canvas, your finished design will be proportionately larger; #14 proportionately smaller.

The design on page 32 is actually only one section of a larger square design formed by repeating the motif four times. Each time the motif is used it is rotated an additional 90°.

It is a good idea to work out a complete, detailed color scheme for the design before beginning a project. You may find it more convenient to put tracing paper over the design and to experiment with colors on the tracing paper. In this way the design in the book will not be ruined if you decide to change the colors.

There are two distinct types of needlepoint canvas, single-mesh and double-mesh. Double-mesh is woven with two horizontal and two vertical threads forming each mesh whereas single-mesh is woven with one vertical and one horizontal thread forming each mesh. Double-mesh is a very stable canvas on which the threads will stay securely in place as you work. Single-mesh canvas, which is more widely used, is a little easier on the eyes because the spaces are slightly larger.

A tapestry needle with a rounded, blunt tip and an elongated eye is used for needlepoint. The most commonly used needle for a #10 canvas is the #18 needle. The needle should clear the hole in the canvas without spreading the threads. Special yarns which have good twist and are sufficiently heavy to cover the canvas are used for needlepoint.

Although there are over a hundred different needlepoint stitches, the one that is universally considered to be "the" needlepoint stitch is the *Tent Stitch,* an even, neat stitch that always slants upward from left to right across the canvas. The stitches fit very neatly next to their neighbors and form a hard finish with the distinctive look that belongs to needlepoint. The three most familiar variations of Tent Stitch are: Plain Half-Cross Stitch, Continental Stitch and Basket Weave or Diagonal Stitch. The choice of stitch has a great deal to do with the durability of the finished project.

Plain Half-Cross Stitch, while it does not cover the canvas as well as the other two variations, provides the most economical use of yarn. It uses about one yard of yarn for a square inch of canvas. The stitch works up quickly, but it has a tendency to pull out of shape, a disadvantage that can be corrected in blocking. This stitch should only be used for pictures, wall hangings and areas that will receive little wear. It must be worked on a double-mesh canvas.

Continental Stitch, since it covers the front and back of the canvas, requires more wool than the Plain Half-Cross Stitch (it uses about 1¼ yards of yarn to cover a square inch of fabric). The stitch works up with more thickness on the back than on the front. As a result the piece is more attractive with better wearing ability. This is an ideal stitch for tote bags, belts, headbands, upholstery and rugs since the padding on the reverse saves wear on the needlepoint. The Continental Stitch also pulls the canvas out of shape, but this is easily corrected by blocking.

The Basket Weave or Diagonal Stitch makes an article that is very well padded and will wear well. It uses the same amount of wool as the Continental Stitch and does not pull the canvas out of shape. Since the stitch is actually woven into the canvas, it reinforces the back. This stitch is especially suited for needlepoint projects that will receive a great deal of wear, such as chair seats and rugs. Its disadvantage is that it lacks maneuverability and is hard to do in areas where there are small shapes or intricate designs.

Plain Half-Cross Stitch: Always work Half-Cross Stitch from left to right, then turn the canvas around and work the return row, still stitching from left to right. Bring the needle to the front of the canvas at a point that will be the bottom of the first stitch. The needle is in a vertical position when making the stitch. Keep the stitches loose for minimum distortion and good coverage.

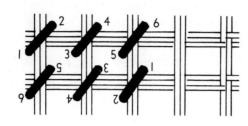

Continental Stitch: Start this design at the upper right-hand corner and work from right to left. The needle is slanted and always brought out a mesh ahead. The resulting stitch is actually a Half-Cross Stitch on top and a slanting stitch on the back. When the row is finished, turn the canvas around and work the return row, still stitching from right to left.

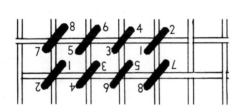

Basket Weave or Diagonal Stitch: Start the Basket Weave in the top right-hand corner (left-handed workers should begin at the lower left). Work the rows diagonally, first going down the canvas from left to right and then up the canvas from right to left. The rows must be alternated properly or a faint ridge will show where the pattern has been interrupted. Always stop working in the middle of a row rather than the end so that you will know in what direction you are working.

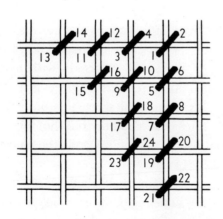

When starting a project, allow at least a 2″ margin of plain canvas around the needlepoint. Bind all the raw edges of the canvas with masking tape, double-fold bias tape or even adhesive tape. There are no set rules on where to begin a design. Generally it is easier to begin close to the center and work outward toward the edges of the canvas, working the backgrounds or borders last. To avoid fraying the yarn, work with strands not longer than 18″.

When you have finished your needlepoint, it should be blocked. No matter how straight you have kept your work, blocking will give it a professional look.

Any hard, flat surface that you do not mind marring with nail holes and one that will not be warped by wet needlepoint can serve as a blocking board. A large piece of plywood, an old drawing board or an old-fashioned doily blocker are ideal.

Moisten a Turkish towel in cold water and roll the needlepoint in the towel. Leaving the needlepoint in the towel overnight will insure that both the canvas and the yarn are thoroughly and evenly dampened. Do not saturate the needlepoint! Never hold the needlepoint under the faucet as this much water is not necessary.

Mark the desired outline on the blocking board, making sure that the corners are straight. Lay the needlepoint on the blocking board, and tack the canvas with thumbtacks about ½″ to ¾″ apart. It will probably take a good deal of pulling and tugging to get the needlepoint straight, but do not be afraid of this stress. Leave the canvas on the blocking board until thoroughly dry. Never put an iron on your needlepoint. You cannot successfully block with a steam iron because the needlepoint must dry in the straightened position. You may also have needlepoint blocked professionally. If you have a pillow made, a picture framed, or a chair seat mounted, the craftsman may include the blocking in his price.

Your local needlepoint shop or department where you buy your materials will be happy to help you with any problems.

87

1

126   85

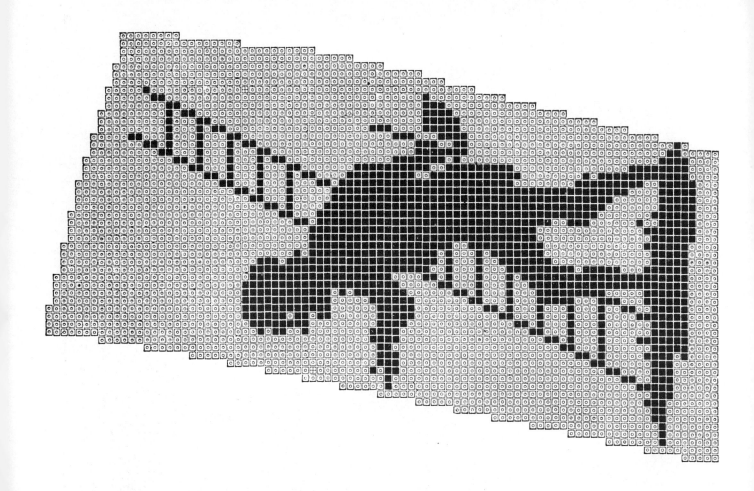

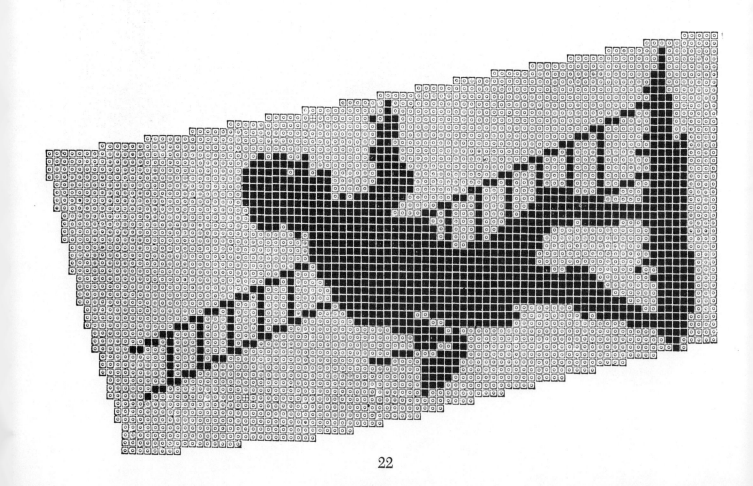

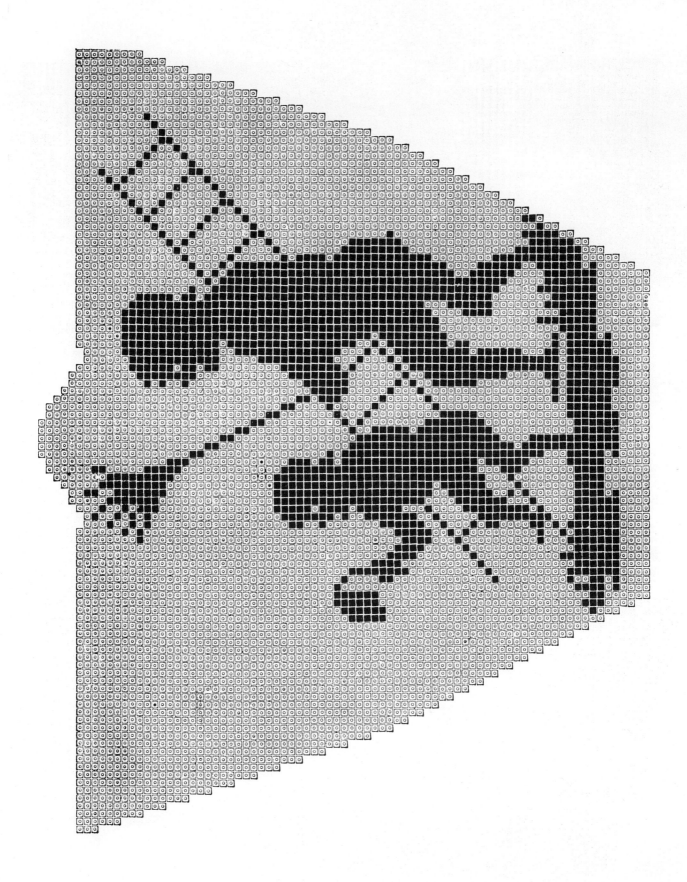

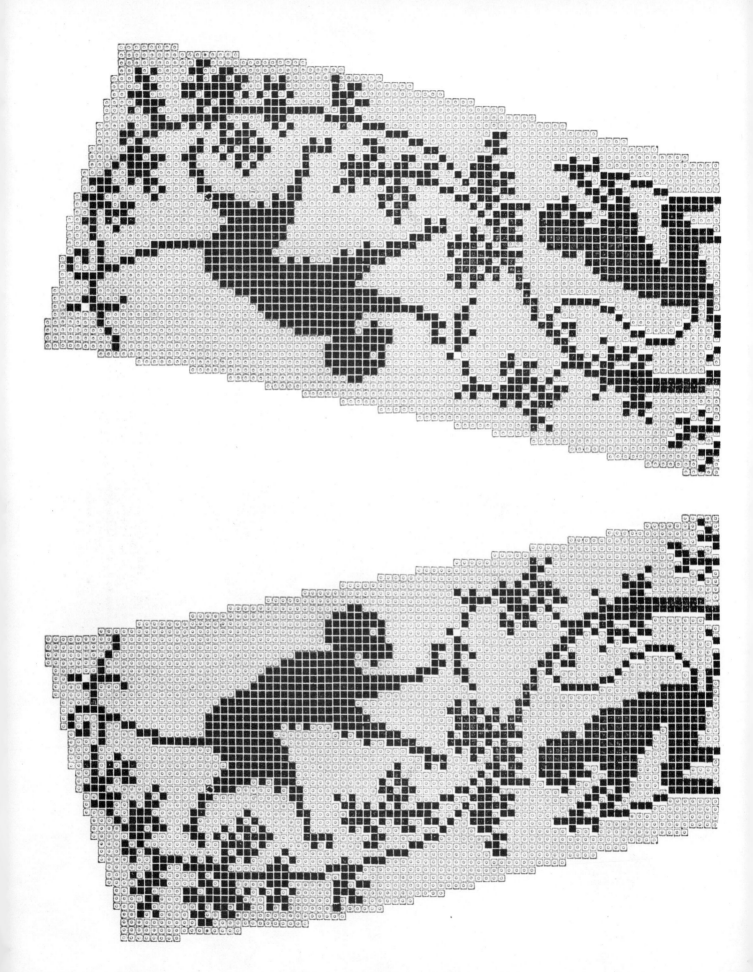

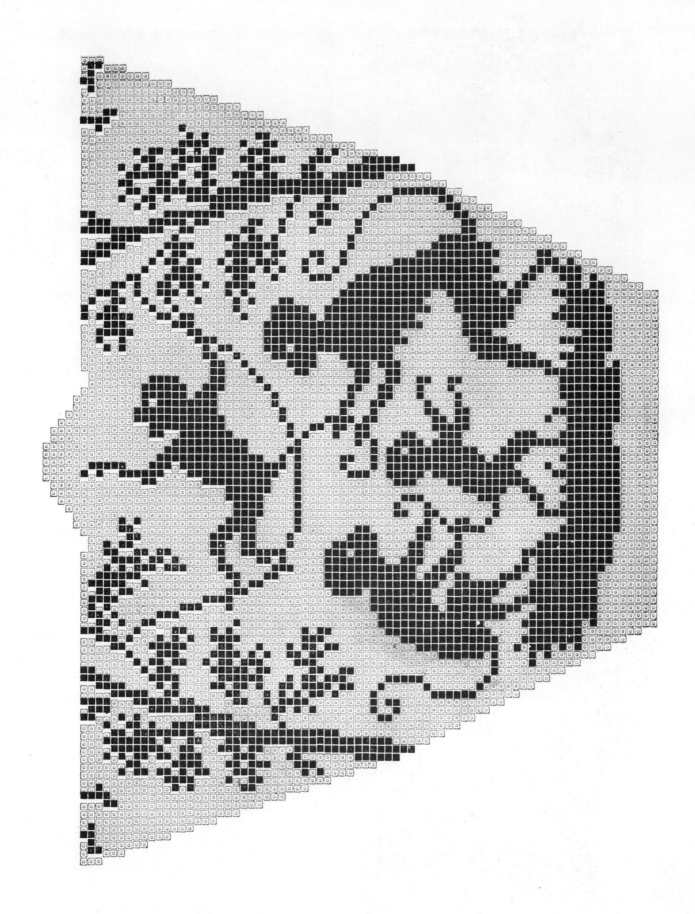

25

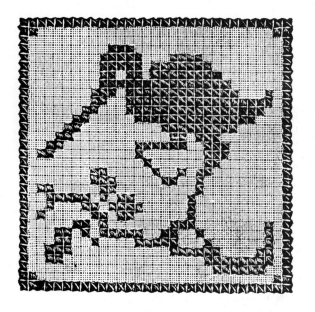
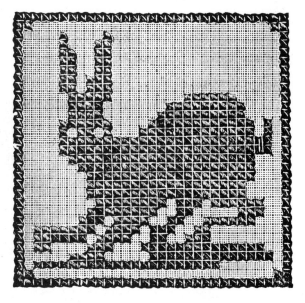

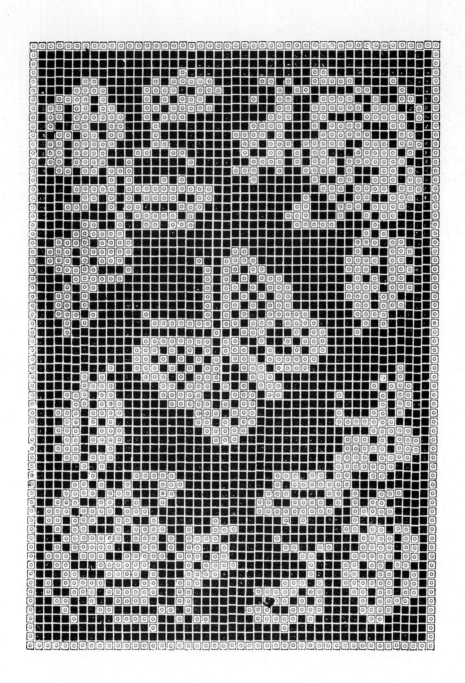

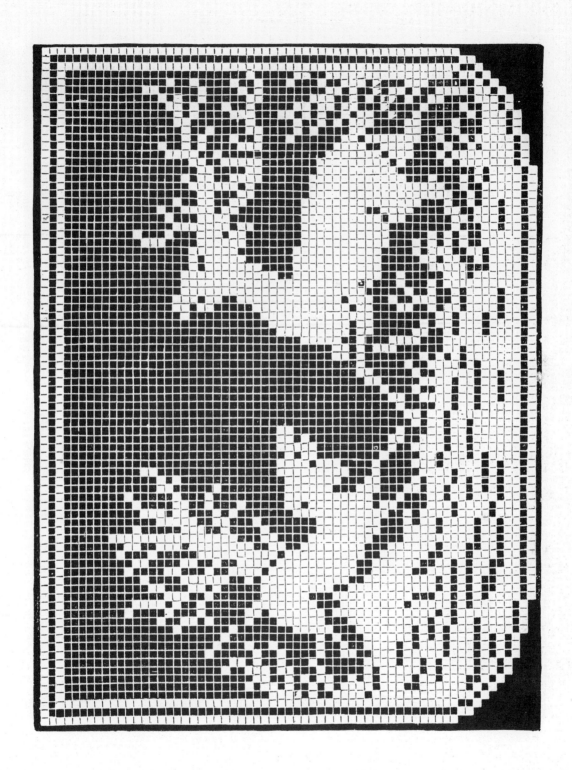

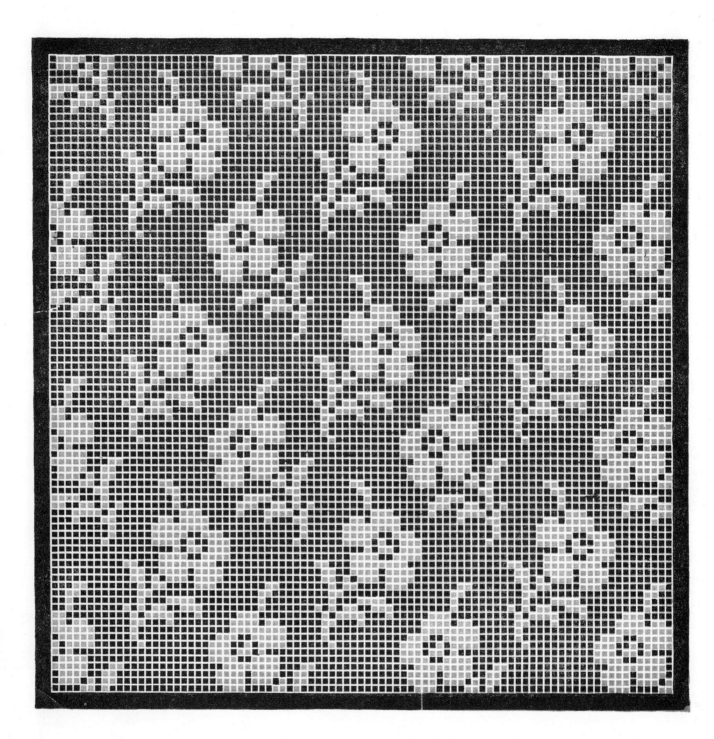

31

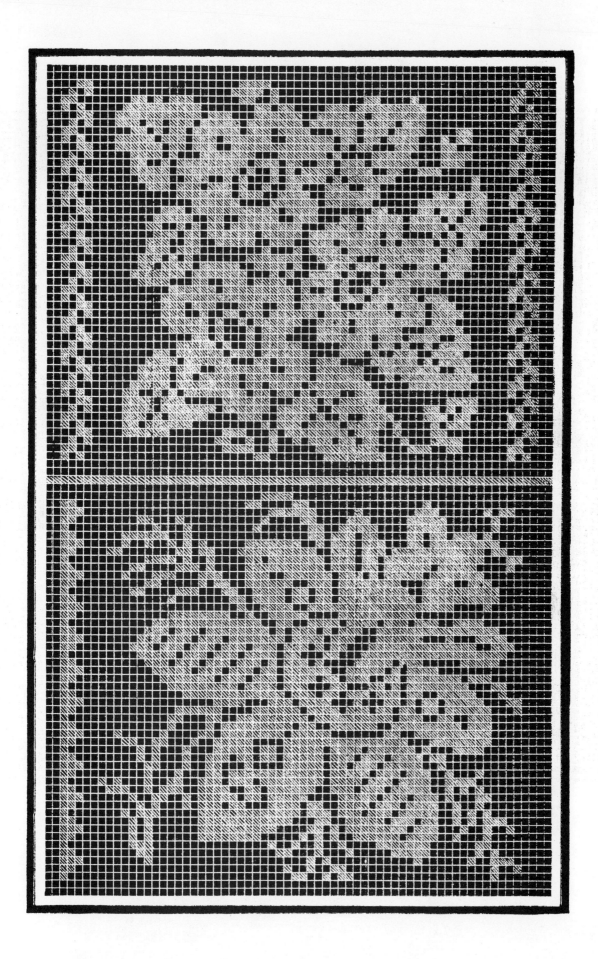

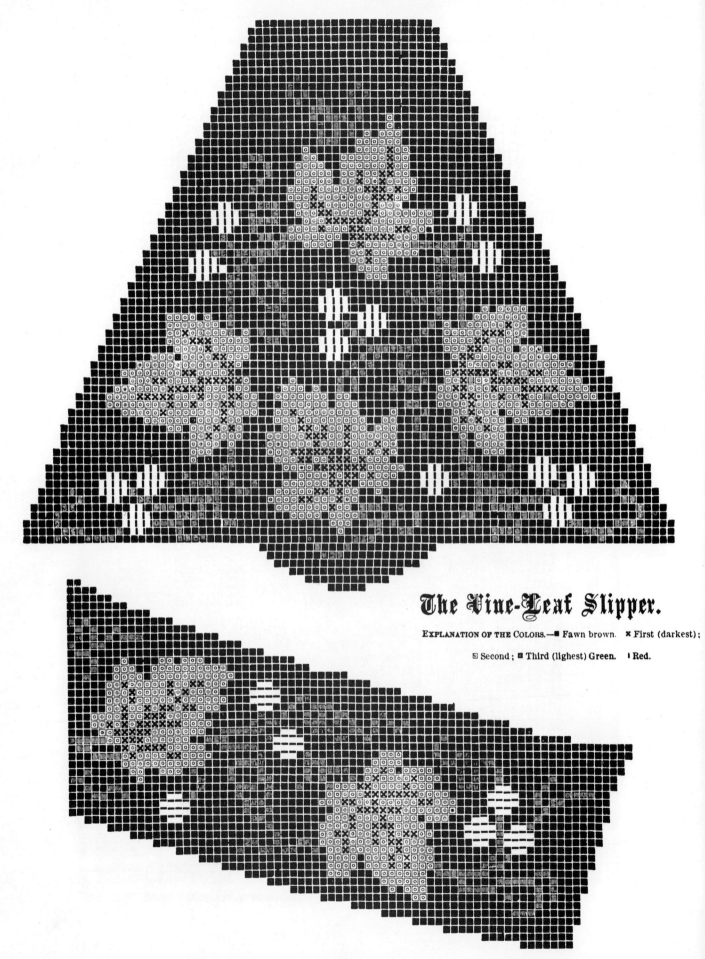

The Vine-Leaf Slipper.

EXPLANATION OF THE COLORS.— ■ Fawn brown.   ✗ First (darkest);

▣ Second ; ▪ Third (lighest) Green.   ∣ Red.

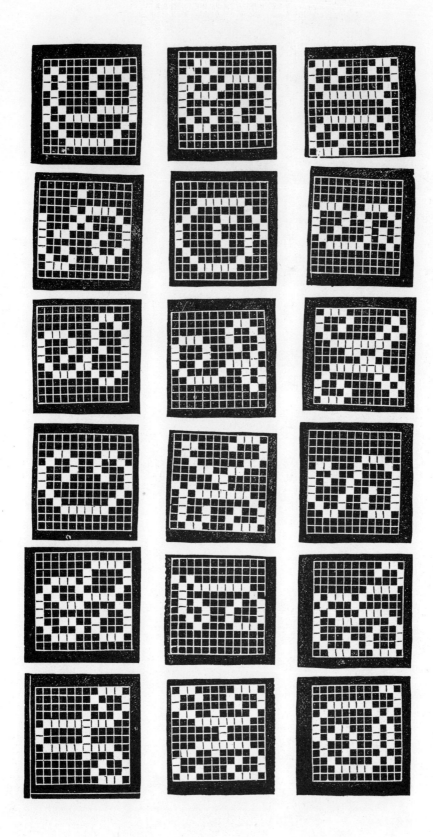

DOVER BOOKS ON NEEDLEPOINT, EMBROIDERY

BASIC NEEDLERY STITCHES ON MESH FABRICS, Mary Ann Beinecke. (21713-2) $3.00

DESIGNS AND PATTERNS FOR EMBROIDERERS AND CRAFTSMEN, Wm. Briggs and Company Ltd. (23030-9) $4.50

HARDANGER EMBROIDERY, Sigrid Bright. (23592-0) $1.50

FRUIT AND VEGETABLE IRON-ON TRANSFER PATTERNS, Barbara Christopher. (23556-4) $1.50

NEEDLEWORK ALPHABETS AND DESIGNS, Blanche Cirker (ed.). (23159-3) $2.25

AMERICAN INDIAN NEEDLEPOINT DESIGNS, Roslyn Epstein. (22973-4) $1.50

DANISH PULLED THREAD EMBROIDERY, Esther Fangel, Ida Winckler and Agnete Madsen. (23474-6) $3.00

PATCHWORK QUILT DESIGNS FOR NEEDLEPOINT, Frank Fontana. (23300-6) $1.50

CHARTED FOLK DESIGNS FOR CROSS-STITCH EMBROIDERY, Maria Foris and Andreas Foris. (23191-7) $2.95

BLACKWORK EMBROIDERY, Elisabeth Geddes and Moyra McNeill. (23245-X) $3.50

VICTORIAN ALPHABETS, MONOGRAMS AND NAMES FOR NEEDLEWORKERS, Godey's Lady's Book. (23072-4) $3.50

VICTORIAN NEEDLEPOINT DESIGNS, Godey's Lady's Book and Peterson's Magazine. (23163-1) $1.75

A TREASURY OF CHARTED DESIGNS FOR NEEDLEWORKERS, Georgia L. Gorham and Jeanne M. Warth. (23558-0) $1.50

GEOMETRIC NEEDLEPOINT DESIGNS, Carol Belanger Grafton. (23160-7) $1.75

FULL-COLOR BICENTENNIAL NEEDLEPOINT DESIGNS, Carol Belanger Grafton. (23233-6) $2.00

FULL-COLOR RUSSIAN FOLK NEEDLEPOINT DESIGNS, Frieda Halpern. (23451-7) $2.25

WHITE WORK: TECHNIQUES AND DESIGNS, Carter Houck (ed.). (23695-1) $1.75

CLASSIC POSTERS FOR NEEDLEPOINT, M. Elizabeth Irvine. (23640-4) $1.50

FAVORITE PETS IN CHARTED DESIGNS, Barbara Johansson. (23889-X) $1.75

CREATIVE STITCHES, Edith John. (22972-6) $3.50

NEW STITCHES FOR NEEDLECRAFT, Edith John. (22971-8) $3.00

PERSIAN RUG MOTIFS FOR NEEDLEPOINT, Lyatif Kerimov. (23187-9) $2.00

CHARTED PEASANT DESIGNS FROM SAXON TRANSYLVANIA, Heinz Kiewe. (23425-8) $2.00

Paperbound unless otherwise indicated. Prices subject to change without notice. Available at your book dealer or write for free catalogues to Dept. Needlework, Dover Publications, Inc., 180 Varick Street, New York, N.Y. 10014. Please indicate field of interest. Each year Dover publishes over 200 books on fine art, music, crafts and needlework, antiques, languages, literature, children's books, chess, cookery, nature, anthropology, science, mathematics, and other areas.

Manufactured in the U.S.A.